DISCOVERING

STEM at the Amusement Park

STEM
▶ in the ◀
Real
World

Cynthia Roby

PowerKiDS press.

New York

Published in 2016 by The Rosen Publishing Group, Inc.
29 East 21st Street, New York, NY 10010

First Edition

Editor: Sarah Machajewski
Book Design: Mickey Harmon

Photo Credits: Cover (amusement park) Bucchi Francesco/Shutterstock.com; cover, pp. 1, 3–4, 6, 8, 10, 12, 14, 16, 18, 20, 22–24 (banner design) linagifts/Shutterstock.com; cover, pp. 1, 4, 8, 10, 12, 14, 16, 20 (logo/caption box) Vjom/Shutterstock.com; p. 5 Caiaimage/Paul Bradbury/Getty Images; p. 7 Marcio Jose Bastos Silva/Shutterstock.com; p. 9 elina/Shutterstock.com; p. 11 dwphotos/Shutterstock.com; p. 13 Poznyakov/Shutterstock.com; p. 15 Raywoo/Shutterstock.com; p. 17 coloursinmylife/Shutterstock.com; p. 18 © iStockphoto.com/Julie Marshall; p. 19 Andrew F. Kazmierski/Shutterstock.com; p. 21 © iStockphoto.com/jjshaw14; p. 22 Dragon Images/Shutterstock.com.

Library of Congress Cataloging-in-Publication Data

Roby, Cynthia, author.
 Discovering STEM at the amusement park / Cynthia Roby.
     pages cm. — (STEM in the real world)
 Includes bibliographical references and index.
 ISBN 978-1-4994-0910-9 (pbk.)
 ISBN 978-1-4994-0912-3 (6 pack)
 ISBN 978-1-4994-0962-8 (library binding)
 1. Amusement parks—Miscellanea—Juvenile literature. 2. Science—Study and teaching (Elementary)—Juvenile literature. I. Title.
 GV1853.2.R63 2016
 791.06'8—dc23
                               2015011913

Manufactured in the United States of America

CPSIA Compliance Information: Batch #WS15PK: For Further Information contact Rosen Publishing, New York, New York at 1-800-237-9932

Contents

Get Ready for an Adventure!

An amusement park is an exciting place to visit. You can spin, twirl, splash, twist, and slide. You can meet your favorite movie characters. You can make new friends. You can try new foods. You can scream if the ride is scary! Did you know you can discover STEM at the amusement park, too?

"STEM" stands for "science, **technology**, **engineering**, and math." They're everywhere in amusement parks. Look closely. Explore and ask questions. See how things around you work.

This family will have a fun day at the amusement park. While enjoying their favorite rides, they can learn about STEM, too!

4

STEM Smarts

This smartphone will help you discover more about STEM while you're having fun at the amusement park.

5

A Heart-Pounding Ride

You've bought your ticket and you're ready to ride the roller coaster. A worker fastens your safety bar. The ride takes off, the cars climb high, and then they race down the track. Everyone screams!

A roller coaster moves by the power of **momentum**. Momentum is **mass** in motion. The momentum that builds as a roller coaster races down the first hill is what carries it around the rest of the track.

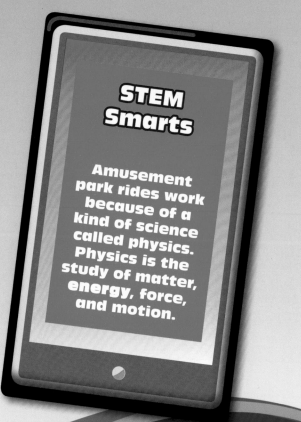

STEM Smarts

Amusement park rides work because of a kind of science called physics. Physics is the study of matter, energy, force, and motion.

6

Roller coasters have two kinds of energy. When it's standing still at the top of a hill, the car has potential, or stored, energy. When the car comes racing down, it has kinetic, or moving, energy.

7

A Jumping Force

If you've ever wanted to feel what it's like to fly, bungee jumping may be the ride for you. You'll wear a harness, or set of straps, that's connected to long cords. Then, take a deep breath and jump! Just as you're about to hit the ground, the bungee cord pulls you back up. You'll bounce up and down until you stop.

Three forces play a part in bungee jumping. The first force is **gravity**. It pulls you toward the ground. The second is **air resistance**. The faster you fall, the more air resistance fights against you. The third is spring force created by the bungee cord.

Bungee jumping may seem scary, but it's safe. Engineers have worked to make sure harnesses and cords can hold enough weight without breaking. They test this **equipment** thousands of times before it can be used in an amusement park.

8

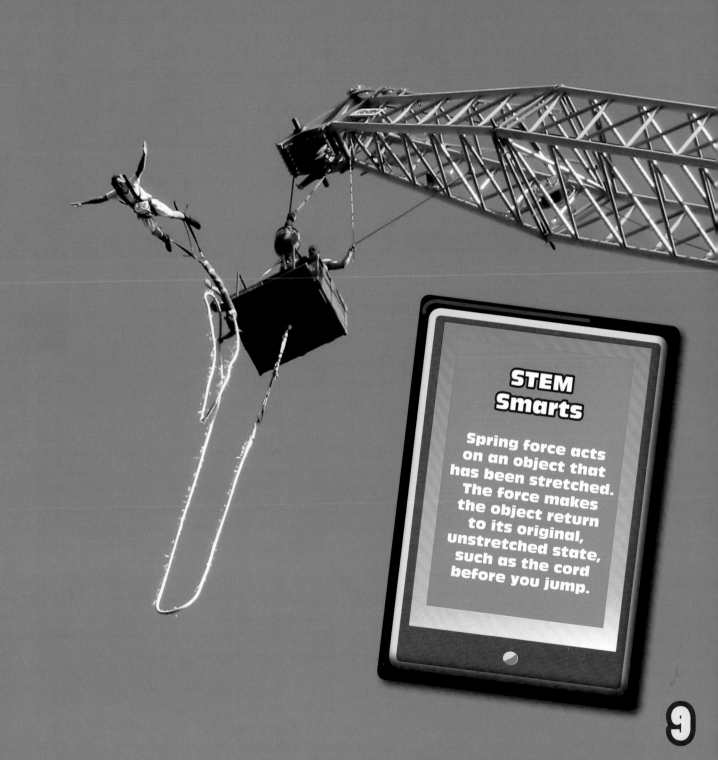

STEM Smarts

Spring force acts on an object that has been stretched. The force makes the object return to its original, unstretched state, such as the cord before you jump.

9

Drive and Crash

Want to spin around, crash into your friends, and drive away safely? Get ready for the bumper cars! A bumper car is a small electric machine. It has a rubber bumper wrapped around it, which **cushions** the car during crashes. Engineers build these cars to be safe and fun.

Bumper cars run on electricity. A wire grid in the ride's ceiling has electric current running through it. The current is carried by a pole that runs from the ceiling to the car. All you have to do is step on the pedal and **steer**!

Your body will get thrown around as your car crashes into things. Make sure to wear a seat belt!

10

11

A Wet Roller Coaster

Are you ready to cool down? Try the water slides! A water slide is like a wet roller coaster—only the seat and safety bar are missing. It uses the same STEM concepts as roller coasters: momentum and gravity.

Climb to the top of the water slide. Sit down, and then push off. The force of the push moves you forward, and gravity pulls you down the slide. As you slide down, you build momentum. Water makes the slide smooth and slippery. This lowers the **friction** between the slide and your raft, which is why you slide fast!

Water-slide technology involves pumps, pipes, and motors. A motor powers a pump, which has a **propeller** inside. The propeller spins and pushes water to the top of the slide. Then, the water exits the pump in a small, constant stream.

STEM Smarts

Let's say a water slide uses 1,000 gallons (3,785.4 L) of water an hour. How many gallons of water does the slide use in an eight-hour day? The answer is 8,000 gallons (30,283.3 L).

13

Carousel Math

The carousel is a very popular ride. The line to get on the ride might be very long. How long do you have to wait? Simple math can help you figure that out.

When you look at the sign near the ride, you see that it holds 25 people. You also know that the ride lasts 5 minutes. This means that for every 25 people, you must wait in line for 5 minutes. Looking around, you see there are fewer than 25 people in front of you. You're next!

If there were 50 people in front of you, you would have to wait 10 minutes to get on the carousel. That's because you would have to wait for 2 groups of 25 people, which would each be on the ride for 5 minutes.

15

To the Top

Have you ever been on a Ferris wheel? If so, you've been a part of science at work, through an idea called "centripetal acceleration." All these big words mean is that you feel lighter at the top of the wheel and heavier at the bottom.

Ferris wheel science depends on math. Engineers and scientists use math equations to figure out how much weight the ride can carry and how much power is needed to move the weight forward, up, and down.

Centripetal acceleration has to do with how an object moves in a circular path. The acceleration is directed inward toward the center of the circle, which affects how heavy or light you feel.

16

STEM Smarts

The first Ferris wheel was invented in 1893. It was built for the Chicago World's Fair. It was 264 feet (80.4 m) tall and carried 38,000 passengers a day.

17

Tricky Games

STEM may help you win or lose a game at an amusement park. Have you ever tried to knock down a stack of cans to win a prize? It's not as simple as it looks.

The cans are stacked in a triangle. You get one toss to knock them over. Most people throw the ball at the center of the triangle, but it doesn't fall! Why? It's because most of the triangle's mass is in its lower half—not the center. Because the mass is uneven, it's hard to knock over the cans with one throw. Aim for the bottom of the stack, and thow hard!

These games are made to trick you! Use your STEM skills to beat the next game you play.

19

Sweet Science

One of the sweetest—and most scientific—parts of an amusement park is cotton candy. Cotton candy is really just sugar that's been turned into something that looks quite different.

The first step in making cotton candy is melting sugar. Heat from a machine breaks apart the sugar crystals and turns them into liquid. The machine spins and throws the liquid sugar against the sides of a bowl, where it cools. The sugar is thrown so hard and cools so quickly that it doesn't have time to harden. What you have instead is light, fluffy cotton candy.

Cotton candy was first called "fairy floss." Can you see why?

21

A Day of Fun

Amusement parks are filled with excitement and discovery. Among all the rides, games, food, and fun, there are also many opportunities to learn. In fact, you may not even feel like you're learning, since amusement parks make STEM seem like an adventure!

An amusement park can be a wide-open and fun-filled classroom. In it, you can discover science, technology, engineering, and math. You don't even have to look far. They're all around you!

Glossary

air resistance: The force of molecules in the air pushing against an object.

cushion: To soften the force of a hit.

energy: The power to do work.

engineering: The use of science and math to improve our world.

equipment: The tools needed to do something.

friction: The force created when one object moves over another.

gravity: The force that pulls an object toward the center of Earth.

mass: The amount of matter an object holds.

momentum: The motion of a moving body, which is measured by its mass and speed.

propeller: An object with blades that turn in a circle in order to power something.

steer: To guide how an object moves.

technology: The way people do something using tools and the tools that they use.

Index

A

air resistance, 8

B

bumper cars, 10

bungee jumping, 8

C

carousel, 14

centripetal
    acceleration,
    16

cotton candy, 20

E

electricity, 10

engineering, 4, 8,
    10, 16, 22

F

Ferris wheel, 16, 17

friction, 12

G

games, 18, 19, 22

gravity, 8, 12

K

kinetic energy, 7

M

mass, 6, 18

math, 4, 14, 16, 22

momentum, 6, 12

P

potential energy, 7

R

roller coaster, 6,
    7, 12

S

science, 4, 6, 16,
    20, 22

spring force, 8, 9

T

technology, 4,
    12, 22

W

water slides, 12, 13

Websites

Due to the changing nature of Internet links, PowerKids Press has developed an online list of websites related to the subject of this book. This site is updated regularly. Please use this link to access the list: www.powerkidslinks.com/stem/park

24